BODY ART

Written by Jean Bennett

Contents

A Tradition	2
Face Paint	4
Body Art	7
War Paint	10
Tattoos	11
Body Art Today	12

A Tradition

Have you ever worn a fake tattoo, had your face painted at a fair, or used makeup to create a scary character for Halloween? If so, you've taken part in the age-old tradition of using body art.

People have been decorating their bodies for thousands of years. Body art was an early form of storytelling. People painted designs on their bodies to share information or tell stories about their lives. These designs might have identified a chief or an elder or a person's tribe, shown that someone was married, or marked other special events in life.

Designs were made using face paint, makeup,
henna, and tattoos – things that are still used
in many cultures today.

Face Paint

Face paint can completely change the way someone looks. Think of a circus clown, whose makeup may include a large mouth and eyes that completely hide the features of the person beneath.

Many cultures use makeup, along with drama, music, and costumes, to tell their traditional stories. Actors wear face paint or makeup to create different characters. In Japanese Kabuki theater, which retells the legends of gods and spirits, the actors have carefully painted faces, and each color has a meaning.

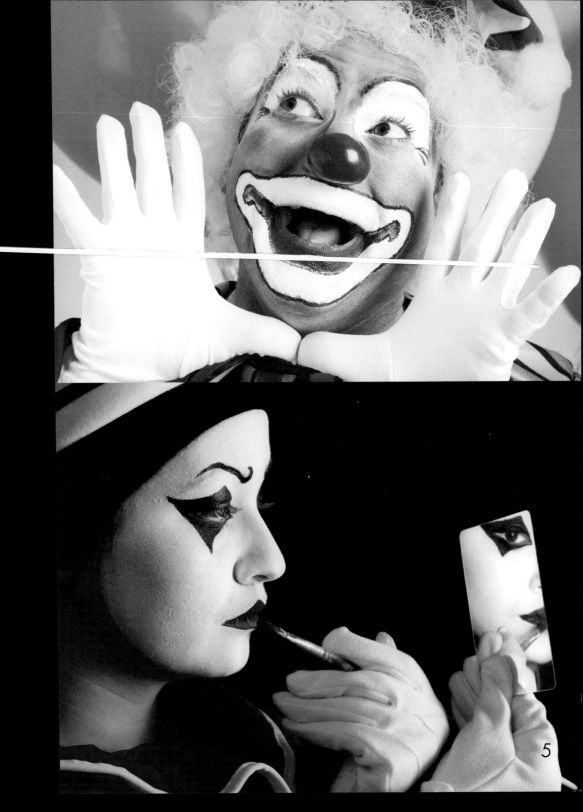

Body Art

There are times when people celebrate who they are and where they came from. Young Masai boys in Africa decorate their bodies with white powder to celebrate becoming an adult. Australian indigenous people also paint markings on their bodies for this reason as well as for funeral ceremonies. The earthy colored designs change from place to place, but they generally show the relationship between people and their environment. Warriors in Papua New Guinea use black body paint to show power, and Brazilian Xinguanos tribesmen wear brightly colored body paint at their important ceremonies.

Weddings are special events when people wear fine clothes and makeup. Brides in India paint their hands and feet with a dye called henna. This process is known as mehndi. After the ingredients have been mixed and the designs applied (which can take up to six hours), the painted areas are left for several hours so that the henna can set. The designs will then last 20 to 30 days.

Wearing a bindi is another Indian tradition that has remained a popular form of body art. Bindi are worn on the forehead, between the eyebrows, for a variety of reasons, such as mourning a death. Traditional bindi were made from ground spices and flowers, but today, many are stickers that can be applied and removed quickly.

War Paint

In many cultures, warriors went into battle with painted faces. The different patterns and colors showed the bravery of the warrior and were meant to terrify the enemy.

Native Americans often painted their faces and bodies to prepare themselves for battle. The patterns and colors varied between tribes, and some were specially chosen by individuals. The red forehead and vertical black lines shown here symbolize rain or tears. Native Americans also painted a handprint on their horse to show that an enemy had been killed during hand-to-hand combat.

Tattoos

All kinds of people wear tattoos today, but they were once linked mainly with sailors, especially tattoos showing anchors, ships, or hearts containing a woman's name.

The connection between tattoos and sailors goes back hundreds of years, when explorers first crossed the oceans looking for new lands and opportunities. The sailors on the whaling ships that visited the South Pacific islands admired the tattoos worn by the local people. Their tattoos were made using fine needle combs or chisels together with soot or vegetable dyes.

Tattoos are designed to be permanent, but sometimes people can change their mind about having a tattoo. Although it's possible to remove some tattoos, it can be a long and painful operation.

Body Art Today

Makeup is the most common form of body art in today's world, although face paint is popular at sports games, where fans paint themselves in their team's colors. Fake tattoos and henna are also popular and easy to use as they wear off over time.

As our communities become more multicultural, the body art from different countries is becoming a more common sight.

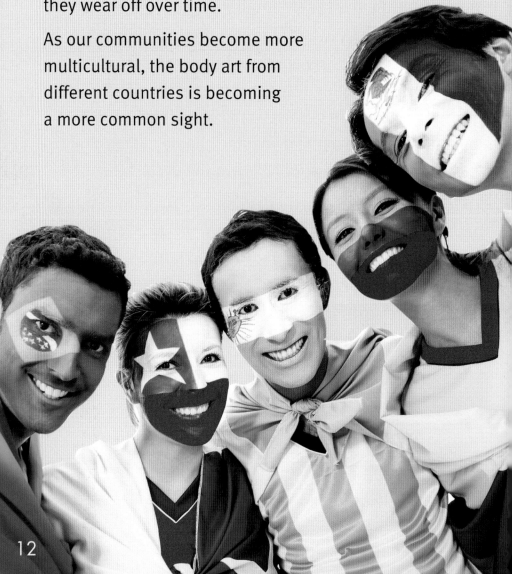